52
Ways to Teach Children to Share the Gospel

Easy-to-do Activities for Ages 5 - 12

Publisher ....*Arthur L. Miley*

Author ....*Barbara Hibschman, M.Ed.*

Managing Editor ....*Carol Rogers*

Assistant Editor ....*Chris D. Neynaber*

Art Director ....*Deborah Birch*

Illustrator ....*Jo Ann Hall*

Proofreader ....*Heather Swindle*

Copyright 1996 • Fourth Printing
Rainbow Books • P.O. Box 261129 • San Diego, CA 92196

#RB36107
ISBN 0-937282-00-6

Dedicated to Jim

*My husband, my pastor,
and my best friend,*

*As a husband for the love, prayers, and encouragement
given while doing this project,*

*As a pastor for his faithfulness in sharing the vision
of reaching our world for Christ throughout his preaching,
teaching, and example,*

*As my best friend for helping in practical ways,
for sharing dreams and goals, and seeing God accomplish
His purposes in and through our lives.*

Barbara Hibschman

52

Ways to Teach Children to Share the Gospel

Easy-to-do Activities for Ages 5 - 12

Introduction

Are you looking for specific material to help your children learn more about spreading the Gospel?

52 Ways to Teach Children to Share the Gospel was written to provide the Christian teacher with a tool to teach children the biblical basis of sharing the Gospel with others. This teacher's resource book can be used in the Sunday school, children's church, VBS, weekday Bible club programs, Christian school classrooms, home schools, day care, and camping programs. The activities inform, instruct, challenge, and nurture the students with the responsibility of being obedient to Christ's last command as found in Matthew 28:18-20, when He said, *"All power is given unto Me in heaven and in earth. Go ye therefore, and teach all nations, baptizing them in the name of the Father, and of the Son, and of the Holy Ghost: Teaching them to observe all things whatsoever I have commanded you: and, lo, I am with you always, even unto the end of the world."* Also, in Mark 16:15, *"Go ye into all the world, and preach the gospel to every creature."*

If the claims and commands of Christ are being taught in our homes, churches, Christian schools, and camps, then we can expect children and teens to respond. These responses need to be nurtured, and the claims of Christ as God's only way of salvation need to be taught.

Each activity has an objective for the teacher, easy-to-follow directions, and a designated age level from ages five through twelve, although some may be adapted for teens and the entire congregation. Also, each activity has a scriptural reference based upon the King James Version or the New International Version of the Bible.

There are a variety of exciting activities including puzzles, crafts, games, maps, songs, choral reading, devotional stories, skits, Bible quizzes, and numerous others which can be duplicated and distributed to each student.

52 Ways to Teach Children to Share the Gospel provides the biblical basis of reaching our world for Christ, starting with going and telling others about Jesus at home, school, and in our neighborhoods. It encourages interest and support of home and foreign missions through prayer and financial giving and suggests practical ways to be a witness and serve the Lord at home.

God bless you in your teaching and make you fruitful for His Kingdom. May the words of Isaiah 55:11 bring hope and encouragement as you teach the truths of God's Word: *"So shall My word be that goeth forth out of My mouth: it shall not return unto Me void, but it shall accomplish that which I please, and it shall prosper in the thing whereto I sent it."*

Ways to Teach Children to Share the Gospel

— Easy-to-do Activities for Ages 5 - 12 —

MEMORY VERSE INDEX

*This activity includes more than one Scripture verse.

52 Ways to Teach Children to Share the Gospel

— Easy-to-do Activities for Ages 5 - 12 —

CONTENTS

*Unless otherwise marked, all Scripture verses are from the King James Version.

Alphabet Code Fun

OBJECTIVE: To give children a biblical basis for sharing the Gospel

Appropriate for ages 6 to 12

God's love is <u>so</u> big. It is for everyone in the whole world. Everyone, everywhere needs to hear the Gospel.

Write the letter of the alphabet that comes after each letter found in the puzzle below. (Exception: The letter A follows the letter Z). You will discover a verse that tells how to have eternal life. This is the message we need to tell people all over the world.

Make a decoder to solve the puzzle. The answer is on page 63.

What you need:
- duplicated puzzle
- marker or pencil
- scissors
- tape
- 6-inch and 4-inch poster board circles
- brass paper fastener

What to do:

1. Your teacher will draw a 3 ¾-inch circle in the center of the smaller circle and will punch a hole in each circle.

2. Fasten the circles with a paper fastener.

3. Use a straight-edge to mark 26 evenly-spaced lines extending from the outer edge of the 3 ¾-inch circle to the outer edge of the 6-inch circle.

4. Print the alphabet in clockwise order on each circle. It doesn't matter where you begin on each circle.

5. To decode the puzzle, line up the A on the outer circle with B on the inner circle. Find the letter under each blank on the outer circle and write the inner circle letter in the blank.

E N Q   F N C   R N   K N U D C

S G D   V N Q K C   S G Z S   G D

F Z U D   G H R   N M D   Z M C

N M K X   R N M   S G Z S

V G N D U D Q   A D K H D U D R

H M   G H L   R G Z K K   M N S

O D Q H R G   A T S   G Z U D

D S D Q M Z K   K H E D

___ ___ ___ ___   3:16 (NIV)
I N G M

2 Mosaic Cross

OBJECTIVE: An eye-catching way to display and reinforce John 3:16

Appropriate for ages 5 to 9

*For God so loved the world
that He gave His one and only Son,
that whoever believes in Him
shall not perish but have eternal life.*
— John 3:16 (NIV)

Everyone needs to hear about God and His love. The colors in this mosaic picture will remind you that Jesus died and lives for all the people of the world. You may want to give it to a friend who is interested in hearing more about Jesus.

What you need:
- 6 x 9-inch piece of black construction paper
- ½-inch strips of red, brown, yellow, black, and white construction paper
- scissors
- glue
- paint brushes (optional)

What to do:
1. Cut each color strip of construction paper into odd shapes of various sizes.
2. Arrange the various colored shapes on the half sheet of black construction paper. Leave a little space between the pieces so that some black will be seen. This will give it the mosaic effect.
3. Glue shapes into place. You may want to use paint brushes to spread the glue over the construction paper.
4. While colored shapes are drying, cut out the John 3:16 cross pattern. Center and glue the cross into place on top of the colored strips.

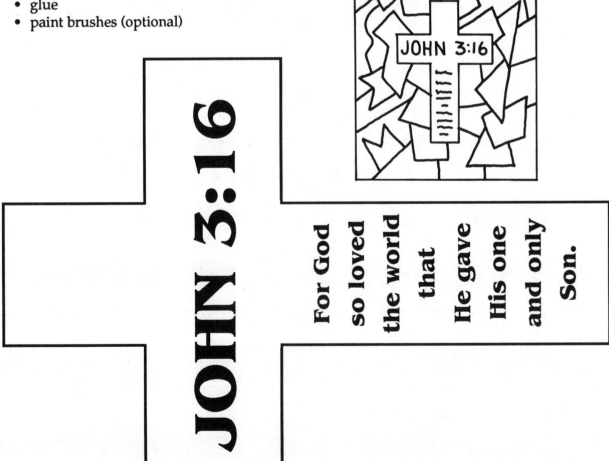

3 His Last Command

OBJECTIVE: To teach children and teens the words of the Great Commission

Appropriate for ages 8 to 12

Missionaries go to spread the Gospel in all the world because they are obeying the Lord's last command. To find the words Jesus spoke to His disciples write the letter of the alphabet that comes before each letter below.

Follow the instructions on page 7 (Alphabet Fun) to make a decoder. To decode the puzzle, line up the A on the outer circle with Z on the inner circle. Find the letter below on the outer circle and write the inner circle letter in the blank.

When the puzzle is finished, draw a picture or write a paragraph describing ways you can obey this command today.

The answer is on page 63.

U I F S F G P S F   H P   B O E

N B L F   E J T D J Q M F T   P G   B M M

O B U J P O T'   C B Q U J A J O H

U J F N   J O   U I F   O B N F   P G

U I F   G B U I F S   B O E   P G   U I F

T P O   B O E   P G   U I F   I P M Z

T Q J S J U'   B O E   U F B D I J O H

U I F N   U P   P C F Z

F W F S Z U I J O H   J   I B W F

D P N N B O E F E   Z P V   B O E

T V S F M Z   J   B N   X J U I   Z P V

B M X B Z T'   U P   U I F   W F S Z

F O E   P G   U I F   B H F.

28:19-20 (NIV)

N B U U I F X

4 Go Ye

OBJECTIVE: Introduces children to ways to travel to people who need to hear the Gospel

Appropriate for ages 5 to 9

*Go ye into all the world,
and preach the Gospel to every creature.*
— Mark 16:15

Jesus told us to go to people who need to hear the Good News of salvation. Color each way a missionary could travel to tell others about Jesus.

You can be a missionary too. Do you know someone who needs to hear about Jesus? Put a circle around the way you would go, or travel, to tell that person the Good News of salvation.

Start praying for that person today. Pray that you will be able to talk about Jesus with that person.

A Thank-You Card

OBJECTIVE: Makes children aware of and thankful for people who have helped them come to know Jesus

Appropriate for ages 7 to 12

Yet to all who received Him,
to those who believed in His name, He gave
the right to become children of God.
— John 1:12 (NIV)

Have you asked God to forgive you of your sins? Have you asked Jesus to be your Savior? If you have, you are God's child.

Who told you how to become God's child? The person who told you about salvation was a missionary to you.

You can make a thank-you card for the person(s) who helped you come to know Jesus as your Savior. Make several cards if you have more than one person to thank.

You can tell others about Jesus, too!

What you need:
• duplicated card pattern from below

• ribbon
• scraps of fabric, felt, lace, yarn, etc.
• construction paper
• scissors
• glue
• glitter
• pen or pencil
• crayons
• markers

What to do:

1. Cut out the pattern below and fold it in half to make a card.

2. Write a short note or verse on the inside of the card.

3. Decorate the card.

4. Give it or send it to that special person who told you about God's Son.

6 Manger Message

OBJECTIVE: To learn Scripture that helps children focus on the message of Christmas

Appropriate for ages 8 to 12

Christmas is a perfect time to talk about why God sent Jesus to earth. It is a good time for us to share this message with family and friends. Jesus was born to be our Savior. He came to die on a tree (cross) for our sins. Everyone needs to hear this message. Through knowing Jesus we have eternal life.

To read the message below, place the correct vowel in each blank. Remember, the vowels are a, e, i, o, u, and sometimes y. Check your answer by looking up the words in the Bible (New International Version).

The answer is on page 63.

H_ H_mself b_r_ __r s_ns _n
H_s b_dy _n th_ tr__, s_ th_t w_
m__ght d___ t_ s_ns _nd l_v_ f_r
r_ght____sn_ss; b_ H_s w___nds
y__ h_v_ b___n h__l_d.

—I Peter 2:24 (NIV)

52 Ways to Teach Children to Share the Gospel

7 Christmas Tree Poem

OBJECTIVE: Reinforces the message of Christmas and encourages the children to share it with others

Appropriate for ages 8 to 12

Share the Gospel by helping to write a Christmas poem and sharing it with someone. Fill in the blanks on the tree. You may choose words from the Word Bank below, or use words of your own. A suggested answer is on page 63.

More Fun Things to Do:
- Draw and color ornaments on the tree.
- Draw gifts under the tree. Write names of people you know who need to hear and receive God's gift of salvation.
- Pray and ask God to help you tell others about His gift of salvation.

Word Bank
sing
Jesus
tree
King
Son
me
voice

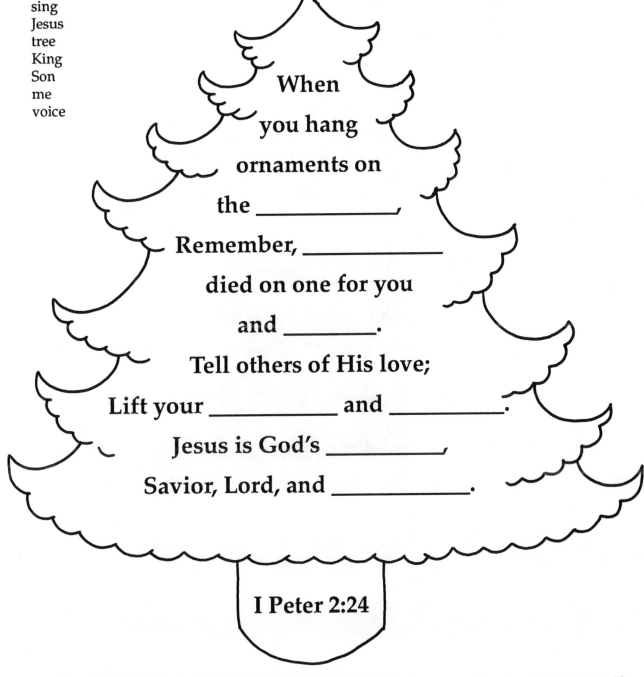

When
you hang
ornaments on
the _____,
Remember, _____
died on one for you
and _____.
Tell others of His love;
Lift your _____ and _____.
Jesus is God's _____,
Savior, Lord, and _____.

I Peter 2:24

Go with the Gospel

OBJECTIVE: To learn Scripture as a biblical basis for sharing the Gospel

Appropriate for ages 9 to 12

Cut out the circle pattern below to make it easier to decipher the message.

Begin by circling the letter G and writing it on the lines below. Skip a letter, circle the next letter, and write it below. Continue around the circle about 1 ¼ times to find out what Mark 16:15 says. Look up the verse in your Bible (King James Version) to make sure you deciphered it correctly. The answer is on page 63.

_____ _____ _____ _____ _____ _____ ,

_____ _____ _____ _____ _____ _____

_____ _____ . — Mark 16:15

9 We Are Messengers

OBJECTIVE: To reinforce the concept that we are sent out from the church to spread the Gospel

Appropriate for ages 6 to 9

They are the messengers of the churches, and the glory of Christ.
—II Corinthians 8:23

Titus was Paul's friend. He and Paul were messengers who were sent out by the church. They told others about Jesus. You can tell others about Jesus, too. One way to start is by inviting people you know to come to your church.

Connect the dots to complete the picture.

On the lines in the picture below, write the names of people you can invite to your church to hear about Jesus. Invite one of those people to come with you to church next week.

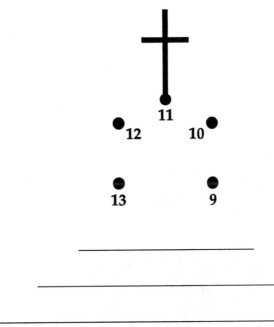

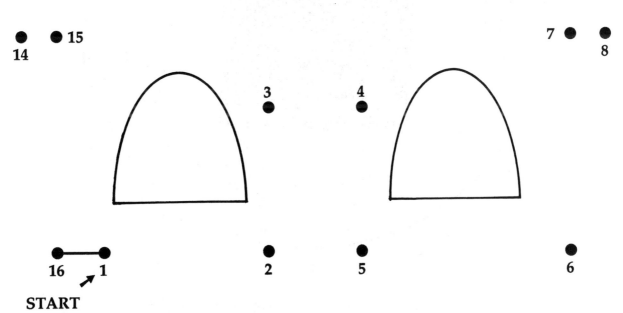

10 Bring a Friend Pop-Up Card

OBJECTIVE: To encourage each child to bring a friend to church

Appropriate for ages 6 to 9

They are the messengers of the churches, and the glory of Christ.
—II Corinthians 8:23

Titus and Paul told others about Jesus. You can help others learn about Jesus, too. Inviting a friend to church is one way to share Jesus with them. Make an invitation to send or give to a friend who needs to hear about Jesus.

Check with your parents to see if your friend could spend the previous night with you or if your parents could pick up your friend on the way to church. You may want to bring an extra Bible for your friend.

What you need:
- two 6 x 8-inch sheets of bright construction paper
- two 6 x 1-inch construction paper strips
- markers or crayons
- scissors
- glue

What to do:
1. Cut out the patterns below (choose a boy or girl runner).
2. Fold two 6 x 8-inch construction paper sheets in half.
3. Make four pencil marks on the folded edge of one construction paper piece, 1 inch from each end and 1 inch from those marks. Cut a 1-inch line at each mark.
4. Fold the cut middle pieces back and press down. Turn the card over and fold from the other side. Open the flaps.
5. Open the card. Press the middle pieces up from behind into box shapes. Pinch up and crease the center fold of the boxes.
6. Spread glue around the edges of the card, and glue it to the other piece of construction paper. Match the center folds. Gently pull the boxes toward you.
7. Make a spring by gluing the two paper strips at right angles. Fold the first strip up over the second. Keep folding the strips across each other until the paper is used up.
8. Glue the top flap and press. Glue the spring inside the card, centered just above the boxes.
9. Glue a hurdle onto each box. Glue the runner onto the spring.
10. Draw a track field around the hurdles.
11. Glue *Jump for Joy...* on the front of the card. Print a message on the track field, and sign your name.

Jump for Joy & Join Us for Church!

Completed Card

11 Fruit of the Spirit

OBJECTIVE: To teach children the fruit of the Spirit, which is needed by all who serve God

Appropriate for ages 8 to 12

As children of God, we are God's messengers. We can tell people about His love. We can explain salvation and how to follow Jesus.

Unscramble the letters in the fruit basket to discover what fruit God's servants need to have.

Then, write the word for each "fruit of the Spirit" on the lines below. The answers are on page 63.

Choose a fruit of the Spirit that you will try to practice this week and circle it.

1. _____

2. _____

3. _____

4. _____

5. _____

6. _____

7. _____

8. _____

9. _____

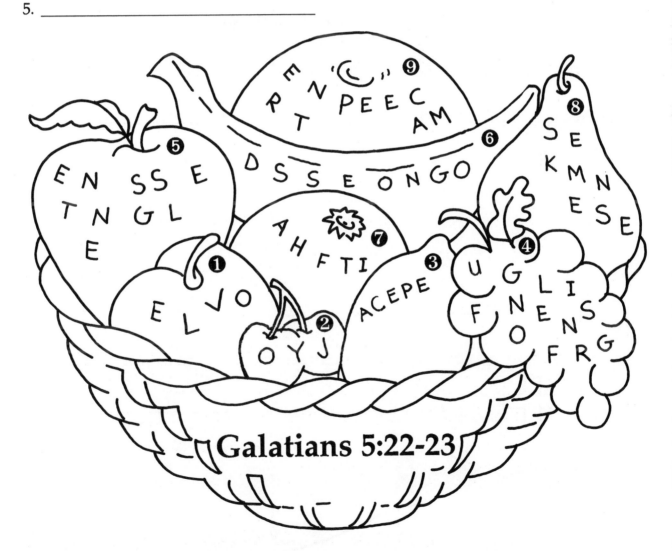

Galatians 5:22-23

52 Ways to Teach Children to Share the Gospel

12 Jesus Is the Way

OBJECTIVE: To help children learn a Bible verse that tells the message of salvation

Appropriate for ages 8 to 12

Jesus is God's only way of salvation. Everyone needs to hear about the Savior. Learn what Jesus said about Himself by crossing out every Q, X, and Z. Then write the remaining letters on the lines below. The answer is on page 63.

QZJZXEXQSQZXUS QQSAQXQIQXZTZH ZZQUQNTXQO HQIZXQM, QZXIZQX QXZAZM QTZXHZEQZ ZQXWXZQAQZXYZ, XTQXZHQEZX ZZQXTZXRQZUTZH, QZXAZQNQZQDXZQ TZHZQXEQZX QZX LZQIQZXZFQZEXZ: QZXNQZXOXZQ ZXMQZXAXXZNQXZ QXZCZXOQZQMQZXEZXQTXZHQXZ UNXZQTXZQOZXQ QZXTHXZEQZ ZXFQZXAQTXZZQZXHZXEQZX RXZ,ZBQZXUQZXTXZ XZBQZXYXZ ZXQMXZQEQZXQZX. XZJZOXQHZXNX 14:6

— — — — — / — — — — — / — — — — /

— — — / — / — — / — — — / — — — , /

— — — / — — — — , / — — — / — — — /

— — — — : / — — / — — — /

— — — — — — / — — — — / — — — /

— — — — — — , / — — — / — — / — — .

— — — — 14:6

13 Memory Verse Bookmark

OBJECTIVE: This craft reinforces the importance of Jesus as Savior and Lord

Appropriate for ages 8 to 12

*Jesus saith unto him,
I am the Way, the Truth, and the Life: no man
cometh unto the Father, but by Me.*
— John 14:6

Missionaries go and tell others about Jesus, and how they can have forgiveness of sins and eternal life through knowing Him. Jesus is the only way to God, so everyone needs to hear about the Savior. Can you say John 14:6 from memory? Knowing it will help when you talk to others about Jesus.

Be a missionary and share this verse. Every time you use your bookmark you will think of John 14:6. Let it remind you to pray for others who need to know Jesus as their Savior and Lord.

What you need:
- plastic canvas
- markers
- large embroidery needle
- various colors of yarn
- construction paper
- scissors
- pen
- hole punch
- ruler

What to do:
1. Cut out the cross and heart patterns.
2. Place the cross pattern on plastic canvas, draw around it, and cut it out.
3. With needle and yarn, weave various colors of yarn in different directions. There is no definite pattern, but your finished work will look like a cross because the plastic canvas is cut that way.
4. Place the heart pattern onto construction paper, trace around it, and cut it out.
5. Print "John 14:6" on one side of the heart, and "Everyone needs to know" on the other side.
6. Your teacher will punch a hole at the top of the cross and another one at the top of the heart.
7. Tie one end of a 4-inch piece of yarn through the hole in the cross. Tie the other yarn end to the hole in the heart.

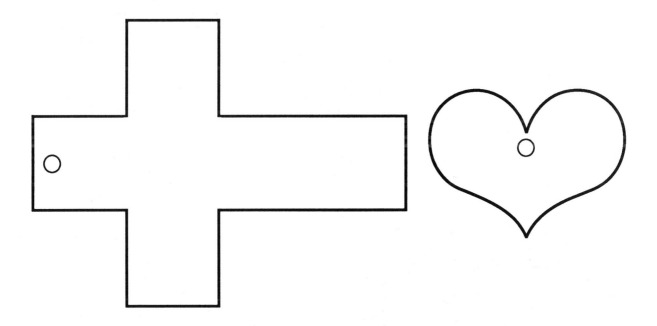

14   John 14:6 Banner

OBJECTIVE: To involve children in a craft that reinforces learning John 14:6

Appropriate for ages 10 to 12

*Jesus saith unto him,
I am the Way, the Truth, and the Life:
no man cometh unto the Father, but by Me.*
— John 14:6

People all over the world are lost in their sins. They are trying to find peace with God in their own way. You can proclaim Jesus as God's only Way of salvation. Jesus is the only Way, the Truth, and the Life.

The whole world needs to know the only way to God. When you look at your finished banner, you will be reminded of John 14:6, and people who need to hear the Good News of salvation. Choose a friend and tell him how he can have his sins forgiven and know God.

What you need:
- a large 12 x 18-inch piece of felt
- thick 24-inch long piece of yarn
- felt scraps in assorted colors
- buttons, yarn, ribbon, lace, beads, fabric scraps, etc.
- white craft glue
- a 14-inch dowel rod, ¼-inch in diameter
- scissors

What to do:
1. Fold one end of the large piece of felt over the dowel rod about 2 ½ inches, and glue the felt edge to the back of the banner

2. Tie the thick yarn to both ends of the dowel rod for hanging.

3. Cut out patterns for letters, face circles, and a cross.

4. Trace the letters, several face circles, and the cross onto the felt and cut them out.

5. Glue them in place on the banner.

6. Use felt scraps, buttons, yarn, etc., to make faces of people. You may have more faces or fewer faces than the pattern shown, depending on how you arrange the faces on your banner.

7. Hang the banner in a place where you will be reminded of John 14:6 and the people you know who need to know Jesus as their Savior.

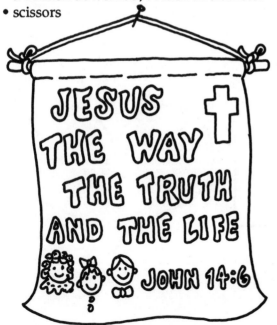

Completed Banner

JESUT
HWAYR
DNLIF
JOHN146

The Good News-Paper

OBJECTIVE: To learn and share the message of salvation

Appropriate for ages 8 to 12

Christ's death and resurrection is the Good News. You can tell the Good News to others.

Fill in the blanks to help you know and share the message of salvation.

God wants you to be His child and live with Him forever.

THE GOOD NEWS

Christ died for our sins…He was buried, and…He rose again the third day according to the Scriptures.
— I Corinthians 15:3-4

For _____ so _____ the _____, that He gave His only begotten _____, that whosoever _____ in Him should not perish, but have _____ _____.

— John 3:16

Sin separates you from God.

For _____ have _____, and come short of the glory of _____.

— Romans 3:23

God is holy, and sin must be punished.

The wages of _____ is _____.

— Romans 6:23

Because of your sin, you need a Savior. Jesus died and rose again to save you from your sins. He is God's only way of salvation.

Neither is there _____ in any other: for there is _____ other name under heaven given among _____, whereby we must be_____.

— Acts 4:12

In John 14:6 Jesus said, "I am the _____, the _____, and the _____: no man cometh unto the Father, but by _____."

But as many as _____ Him, to them gave He power to become the _____ of God, even to them that _____

on His name.

— John 1:12

How can you become God's child and be saved from sin? By praying to God. Ask Him to forgive your sins. Thank Him for sending Jesus to die on the cross for you. Ask Jesus to come into your heart to be your Savior and Lord.

If you have prayed, and asked forgiveness for your sins, and asked Jesus into your heart, you are His child. You have eternal life.

God hath given to us _____ _____, and this life is in His _____. He that hath the Son hath _____; and he that hath not the _____ of God hath not life.

— I John 5:11-12

16 Salvation Bible Verse Quiz

OBJECTIVE: To teach and review Bible verses about salvation

Appropriate for ages 7 to 12

You can share God's Word with someone who doesn't know about Jesus. This quiz will help you learn some verses to share.

Divide the class into two teams. Form two single lines facing the teacher. The teacher says a Bible reference and the first player in each line tries to find it. They cannot receive help from other players. The first person who finds it, reads it aloud. When he is finished he goes to the back of his line and sits down. The player who didn't find the verse goes to the back of the line and waits his turn for another chance. Continue this procedure until all the members of one team are sitting. That team wins.

Salvation Verses

For God so loved the world, that He gave His only begotten Son, that whosoever believeth in Him should not perish, but have everlasting life. — John 3:16

For all have sinned, and come short of the glory of God. — Romans 3:23

For the wages of sin is death; but the gift of God is eternal life through Jesus Christ our Lord. — Romans 6:23

Neither is there salvation in any other: for there is none other name under heaven given among men, whereby we must be saved. — Acts 4:12

Jesus saith unto him, "I am the Way, the Truth, and the Life: no man cometh unto the Father, but by Me." — John 14:6

But as many as received Him, to them gave He power to become the sons of God, even to them that believe on His name. — John 1:12

Behold, I stand at the door, and knock: if any man hear My voice, and open the door, I will come in to him, and will sup with him, and he with Me. — Revelation 3:20

He that hath the Son hath life; and he that hath not the Son of God hath not life. — I John 5:12

For I delivered unto you first of all that which I also received, how that Christ died for our sins according to the Scriptures; And that He was buried, and that He rose again the third day according to the Scriptures. — I Corinthians 15:3-4

Another Fun Thing to Do:

• To help you find the books of the Bible, try doing a little exploration. Which book do you think you will find if you open your Bible in half? *(Psalms)* Try it. What if you open the back half of your Bible in half? *(Matthew)* The front half? *(I Samuel)* Continue opening your Bible in eighths, then sixteenths, as you guess which book of the Bible you will find.

17 Psalm of Gladness

OBJECTIVE: To learn a psalm of gladness and to think of two ways to serve God with joy

Appropriate for ages 8 to 12

A psalm is also a song. David wrote many psalms to praise God. Use the code in the smile to decipher the gladness message from Psalm 100:1- 2 (1=G, 2=L, etc.). The answer is on page 62.

After you solve the puzzle, list two ways you can serve the Lord with joy and gladness today.

M __ k __ __ j o y f u __ __ o i __ __ u __ t o t h __ __ o r __,
   3   6   3   2   5   7 6   5   6   2   4

__ __ __ y __ __ __ __ __ __ __ __ r v __ t h __ __ o r __
3 2 2   6 2 3 5 4 7 7 6 6   6 2 4

w i t h __ __ __ __ __ __ __ __
        1 2 3 4 5 6 7 7

— Psalm 100:1-2

I can serve the Lord with gladness today:

1. _____

_____

_____

2. _____

_____

_____

_____

52 Ways to Teach Children to Share the Gospel

18 Acts 4:12 Body Rhythm

Appropriate for ages 6 to 12

Missionaries go and tell that Jesus is God's only way of salvation. The whole world needs to know this message. Be a missionary and share the news of Acts 4:12 with a friend.

S = Snap fingers on both hands
C = Clap hands together
K = Hit knees with palms of hands
F = Stamp both feet
V = Raise hands
ALL CAPITAL LETTERS = Louder on this word

Neith-er is there SAL-VA-TION
K   K C   C   S   S   S

in an-y oth-er:
C F F F

for there is none oth-er name
S   C   S   C   C   S   K

und-er heav-en giv-en a-mong men,
F F   K   K   C   C K   K   C

where-by we must be SAVED.
F   F   C   C   S   V

Acts 4:12
C K C

19 Before I Come Back Skit

OBJECTIVE: To learn about obedience to God's Word.

Appropriate for ages 8 to 12

Go ye into all the world, and preach the gospel to every creature.
— Mark 16:15

Characters: Mother, Christy, Aggie

Props: dust rag, vacuum cleaner, paper towels, books, bottle of glass cleaner, toys spread all over the floor, a pile of clothes in a corner

Scene 1: Christy and Aggie are sitting on the floor looking at books. Mother appears at the door.

Mother: Christy, before I come back from the grocery store, I want you to clean your room.

Christy: Well . . . okay. Aggie and I were going to ride our bikes to the park. May we go after I finish cleaning my room?

Mother: Yes, but wait until I come back before you leave.

Christy: Okay, see you later!

Mother: I'll be back soon.

Mother exits. Christy starts picking up toys, clothes, etc.

Aggie: Let's surprise your Mom and do a real good job. It won't be hard if we work together.

Aggie and Christy pick up clothes, dust, vacuum, clean the mirror or window, etc.

Scene 2: 45 minutes later

Aggie: The room smells so good and clean.

Christy: She should be home soon. Wait! I hear the car now!

Mother enters the room

Christy: We're finished, Mom. Do you like it?

Mother: It looks great! You even cleaned the mirror. You did a SUPER job. I'm proud of you!

Christy: Thanks, Mom. We worked hard to get everything done before you came back. May we ride our bikes now?

Mother: Sure, but be back in time for supper.

Christy and Aggie exit one way, and Mother exits the opposite way.

Answer the following questions by filling in the blanks. Some may have more than one correct answer.

1. Mother gave Christy a job, or a responsibility. Christy was told to _____ her room.
2. Christy had to do this while _____ was away at the store.
3. Aggie _____ Christy get the job done.
4. Christy _____ mother by doing what she was asked to do.
5. Mother was _____ with what Christy did.
6. God gives us responsibilities in His Word, the _____.
7. God is pleased when we _____ His commands.
8. One of the commands Jesus gave was to tell everyone in the world the Good News of the _____.

20 Jesus' Last Command

OBJECTIVE: To learn the importance of obeying Jesus' last command

Appropriate for ages 8 to 12

Read Mark 16:15-20. Jesus is about to ascend (go back up) to heaven. He will come back, but before He does, He gives His disciples a certain job to do.

This was Jesus' last command. Answer the questions below to find out more about this important charge.

1. What are Jesus' disciples supposed to do while He is away? Write Mark 16:15 in the blanks.

   _____

   _____

   _____

2. The command is given to those who follow Jesus today, too. Now, it is our job, our responsibility to do this before He comes back.

   Where are we to go? _____

   What are we to do? _____

   _____

Many people have asked if that means we are all to become preachers or foreign missionaries. Not necessarily. Some people are preachers and some are foreign missionaries, but others become teachers, doctors, nurses, pilots, church planters (missionaries who start churches) radio and TV personnel, Bible translators, etc.

Business people and politicians also can work to tell others about God and His love for them. God sent His Son, Jesus, to die for our sins so we can have eternal life. Going into all the world is taking the Gospel overseas and across the street. It is sharing the news about Jesus with others.

3. What are you doing right now that shows you are obeying Mark 16:15?

   _____

   _____

   _____

Jesus said in John 14:15 (NIV), "If you love Me, you will obey what I command."

Prayer Time:
Ask the Lord to help you obey and share His Word with others.

21 Work Before Night Story

OBJECTIVE: A story to help children understand the value of one life for eternity

Appropriate for ages 6 to 12

As long as it is day, we must do the work of Him who sent me. Night is coming, when no one can work.
— John 9:4 (NIV)

Eleven-year-old John walked along the Florida seashore enjoying the sunset. The cool moist sand felt good as it squished between his toes. As he walked he heard a strange noise. It sounded like someone, or something, was hurt. He ran toward the sound and found a baby sperm whale about three feet long lying on the sand. It was bleeding.

It must have got caught in a boat propeller, he thought.

"Hey, Dad, Mom, and Christy, come and help!" he called to his family.

John and his family worked hard to dig a little canal with their hands so the water could get to the wounded animal. They had to work fast. Soon it would be dark.

"Animals beach themselves because they think they will die," said Dad.

"Look, there's a lifeguard. I'll go get him. Maybe he can help us," said Mom.

The life-guard called an ambulance for sea animals, and within minutes the baby sperm whale was on his way to a marine-life hospital.

Later, a man passed by and said to John, "You sure worked hard to save one little whale. I live here, and I see plenty of dead animals that have beached themselves, but it looks like you might have gotten to this one just in time."

"I sure hope so. Maybe now he has a chance to live."

Today there are more than five billion people on the earth. Just think, Jesus died for each and every person.

Just as John and his family worked hard to save a baby sperm whale, the Lord wants us to work hard to bring eternal life to others.

Do you know someone who doesn't know that Jesus died for his sins? Or someone who doesn't realize that he can have eternal life? Write his or her name here: _____

Prayer Time:

Dear God, thank You for eternal life through Jesus. Help me to tell others about Him. Help me to remember to pray for _____.

I pray _____ will come to know Jesus as Savior. Use me to lead this person to You. In Jesus' name I ask this.

Amen.

52 Ways to Teach Children to Share the Gospel

22 | Missions News Reporter

OBJECTIVE: To help children learn facts about missionaries and their prayer needs

Appropriate for ages 8 to 12

He that hath the Son hath life.
— I John 5:12

Pretend you are a newspaper reporter. During your missions conference, or any other time a missionary visits, interview him or her and report back to class. You can get some of the answers for these questions by reading the information from church newsletters, bulletins, and magazines or from your pastor.

If you do not have a missionary visiting your church, interview a teacher or pastor or another person in your church whose vocation involves sharing the Gospel.

Missions Interview Questions

1. What is your name? _____
   Are you married or single? _____
   Do you have any children? _____
   If so, what are their names and ages? _____
   _____

2. What is the name of the country (city, church, or organization) where you serve?
   _____

3. How many years have you served there? _____

4. What type of work do you do? _____
   _____
   _____

5. How old were you when you were called to this profession? _____

6. Do you have a prayer request you could share? Our class would like to pray for you.
   _____

7. Would you share a promise from God or a Scripture passage that is special to you?
   _____
   _____
   _____

23 World-Wide Word Search

OBJECTIVE: Gives children a global view of sharing the gospel and missions

Appropriate for ages 6 to 12

Matthew 28:19-20 is known as "The Great Commission." Jesus commands His disciples to take the Gospel into all the world. Duplicate the map on pages 32 and 33.

There are seven masses of land called conti-nents on the earth. Can you find them in the word search? Circle those you find, reading down, across, diagonally, and backwards. As you find them, color them (or highlight their names) on the map. The word search answers are on page 63.

```
X A U S T R A L I A B D E
T H M W R Q I O P Z V A U
W Z A W A U P L N W Q S R
L V C I I W E U I K D A O
A B Q E S Z N I R S Y A P
N O R T H A M E R I C A E
S E I J G S D Q T I X Q H
A C E U I P W B R S C M W
X N Q T Y S H F A E I C B
J S F A N T A R C T I C A
A C I R E M A H T U O S W
```

24 The Good News Song

OBJECTIVE: To learn a Gospel song and to share it with others

Appropriate for ages 5 to 9

You must be born again.
— John 3:7 (NIV)

You can sing songs about salvation so your friends will hear the Gospel message that Jesus saves from sin. Teach them this song so they will hear the Good News of salvation.

Singing is one way to show joy and gladness. When you tell the Good News and others come to know Jesus as their Savior, you are serving the Lord with gladness.

The Good News Song

52 Ways to Teach Children to Share the Gospel

25 World Harvest Map

OBJECTIVE: Gives children a global view of sharing the gospel and missions

Appropriate for ages 6 to 12

Ask the Lord of the harvest, therefore, to send out workers into His harvest field.
— Matthew 9:38 (NIV)

.Jesus commanded His disciples to take the Gospel into all the world. Missionaries travel around the world spreading the Gospel. They need your prayers and encouragement to keep going when things get difficult.

Find the names and countries of several missionaries your church supports. Use the map on pages 32 and 33 to locate their countries on the continents shown. Write the name of the country when you find it. Then, choose a missionary and write him or her a note of support.

What you need:
- duplicated map from pages 32 and 33
- letter-size manila file folder
- scissors
- gold star stickers
- crayons or markers
- glue
- paper
- pencils
- envelopes
- postage stamps

What to do:
1. Cut out the map. For durability, glue it onto the inside of a letter-size manila file folder.
2. Put a gold star in each of the countries where you know a missionary. Then, put a gold star where you live.
3. Use crayons or markers to draw lines from your home to the missionaries you (and your church) support with prayers, letters, and offerings.
4. Cut out the memory verse box below and glue it onto the map (or on the outside of the file folder).
5. Choose a missionary and write him or her a letter of encouragement. Tell a few things about yourself and let the missionary know that he or she is in your prayers.

You are a witness for Jesus where you live. People should be able to tell that you are a Christian by your words and actions. Think of one especially kind action you can do this week to help others know that you are a Christian.

Ask the Lord of the harvest, therefore, to send out workers into His harvest field.
— Matthew 9:38 (NIV)

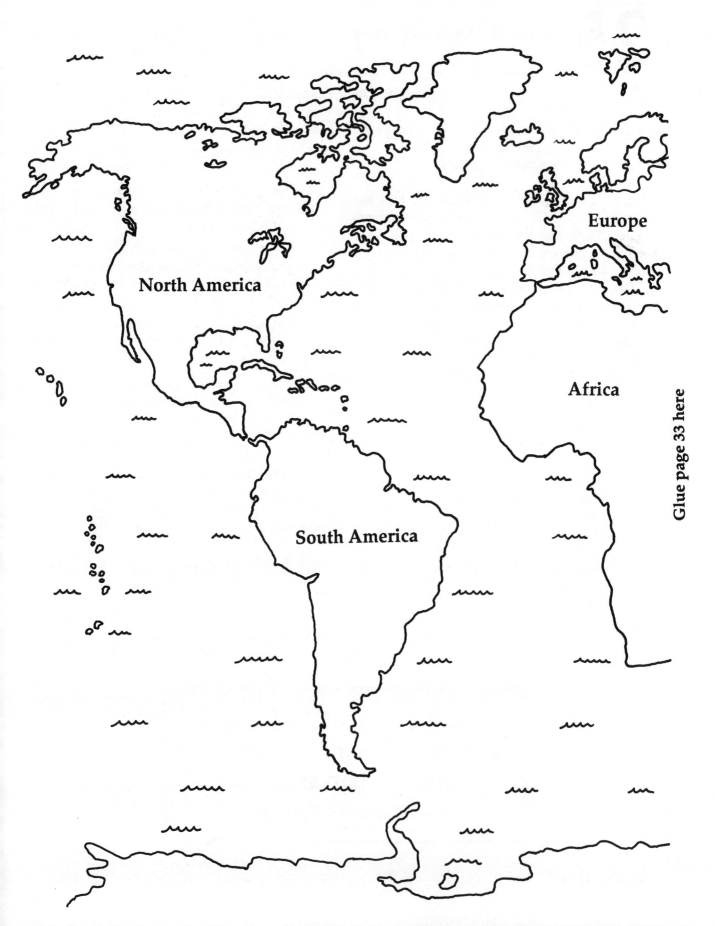

North America

Europe

Africa

South America

Glue page 33 here

52 Ways to Teach Children to Share the Gospel

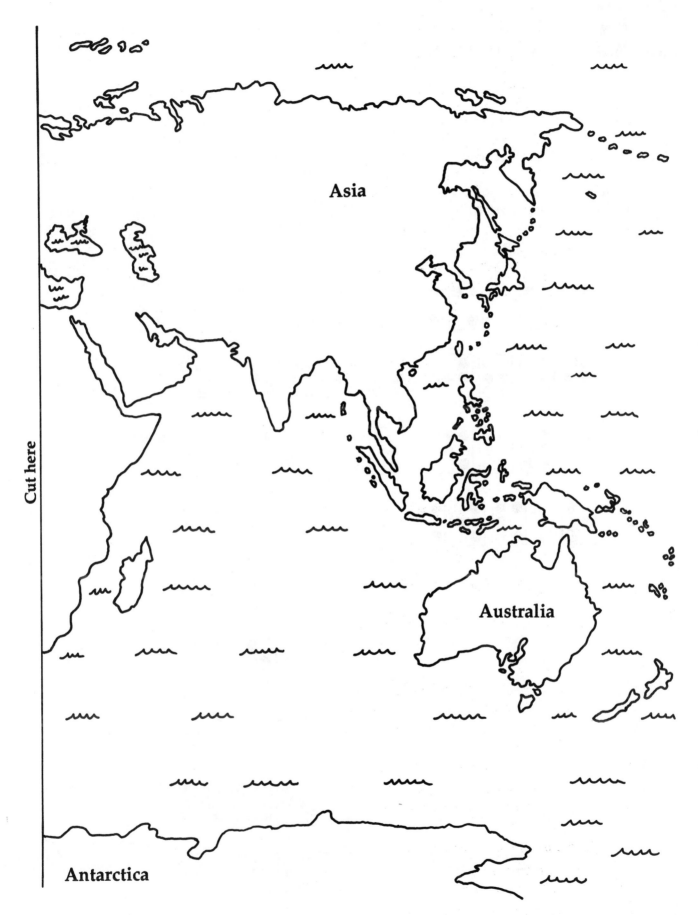

Asia

Australia

Cut here

Antarctica

26 Sent by Jesus Braille Code

OBJECTIVE: To teach Scripture that shows missionaries are sent by the authority of Jesus Christ

Appropriate for ages 8 to 12

Jesus sends us to go and tell others the message of salvation. Use the braille alphabet to decode John 20:21. Write the correct letter above each box.

When you are finished, look up the verse in your Bible (King James Version) to check your solution.

The answer is on page 63.

More fun things to do:

- Take a thumbtack and prick the back side of the solid dots. Then, see if you can read the verse by closing your eyes and "reading" with your fingers.
- Give a copy of the code to a friend. Show him or her how to solve it. Then, tell that person what the passage means.

Code Key

a	b	c	d	e	f

g	h	i	j	k	l

m	n	o	p	q	r

s	t	u	v	w	x

y	z

52 Ways to Teach Children to Share the Gospel

Missionary Psalm Reading

OBJECTIVE: To learn Scripture that gives children a biblical basis for sharing the Gospel

Appropriate for ages 6 to 12

Divide the class into two seating or standing arrangements: boys on one side and girls on the other. Then, select two solo readers and read Psalm 67 as a choral reading.

Psalm 67 is sometimes called a missionary psalm, because it speaks of God's ways being made known in all the nations of the earth.

GIRLS: God be merciful unto us, and bless us; and cause His face to shine upon us.

BOYS: That Thy way may be known upon earth, Thy saving health among all nations.

ALL: Let the people praise Thee, O God; let all the people praise Thee.

SOLO 1:   O let the nations be glad and sing for joy: for Thou shalt judge the people righteously, and govern the nations upon earth.

ALL: Let the people praise Thee, O God; let all the people praise Thee.

SOLO 2:   Then shall the earth yield her increase; and God, even our own God, shall bless us.

ALL: God shall bless us; and all the ends of the earth shall fear Him.

More Fun Things to Do:
- Either read or memorize Psalm 67 and present it in Junior Church, in another Sunday school class, or in a worship service to the entire congregation.
- Sometimes reading aloud can become so routine we forget to pay attention to the meaning of the words. After reading Psalm 67 aloud, describe the meaning of the psalm in your own words. Read the psalm again silently and write down any key words or ideas that seem to be especially important.

28 Pray with Understanding

OBJECTIVE: To develop an awareness of the needs of foreign missionaries in order to promote prayer support.

Appropriate for ages 8 to 12

For this reason, since the day we heard about you, we have not stopped praying for you and asking God to fill you with the knowledge of His will through all spiritual wisdom and understanding.
— Colossians 1:9 (NIV)

When missionaries go to a foreign country, they are faced with many adjustments and needs.

You can serve the Lord right now by praying for them as they share the Gospel.

The words below suggest several problems and obstacles that missionaries often encounter in their travels.

Print the following words in alphabetical order on the lines below. The answers are on page 64.

TRAVEL   LANGUAGE
HEALTH   LONELINESS
SAFETY IN DANGER   CULTURE
RELATIONSHIPS WITH OTHERS CLIMATE
BIBLE READING AND PRAYER

1. _____
2. _____
3. _____
4. _____
5. _____
6. _____
7. _____
8. _____
9. _____

Write the name of a missionary you can pray for this week:

_____

Name a person in your town you can share the Gospel with this week:

_____

29 Bear Each Other's Burdens Puzzle

OBJECTIVE: To remind children to bear the burdens of others in prayer

Appropriate for ages 5 to 9

Bear ye one another's burdens.
— Galatians 6:2

To bear one another's burdens means to pray for and care about other people. This bear puzzle will help you remember to pray for the problems of missionaries, teachers, and people sharing the Gospel. When you pray for them you are obeying God's Word from Galatians 6:2.

Another fun thing to do:

- Give the puzzle to a friend and let her put it together. When it's completed, explain the meaning of Galatians 6:2. Look it up in the Bible if you don't remember the words. Then, say a short prayer with your friend.

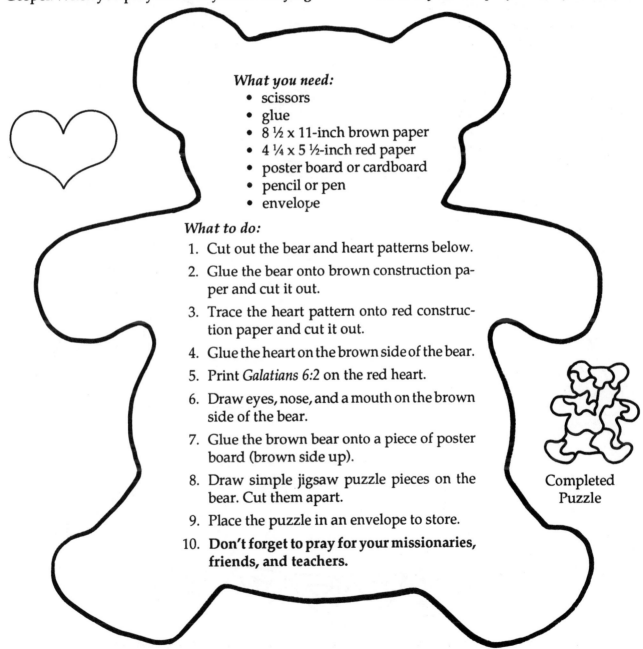

What you need:
- scissors
- glue
- 8 ½ x 11-inch brown paper
- 4 ¼ x 5 ½-inch red paper
- poster board or cardboard
- pencil or pen
- envelope

What to do:

1. Cut out the bear and heart patterns below.

2. Glue the bear onto brown construction paper and cut it out.

3. Trace the heart pattern onto red construction paper and cut it out.

4. Glue the heart on the brown side of the bear.

5. Print *Galatians 6:2* on the red heart.

6. Draw eyes, nose, and a mouth on the brown side of the bear.

7. Glue the brown bear onto a piece of poster board (brown side up).

8. Draw simple jigsaw puzzle pieces on the bear. Cut them apart.

9. Place the puzzle in an envelope to store.

10. **Don't forget to pray for your missionaries, friends, and teachers.**

Completed Puzzle

30 God Cares for Us

OBJECTIVE: To learn Scripture that teaches of God's protection and care in times of danger

Appropriate for ages 6 to 10

Find Psalm 91:11 in your Bible, then write it in the blanks below. This verse brings hope and comfort to missionaries when they are afraid or faced with danger.

This is a good verse to memorize and remember when you are afraid and need God's protection. Remember, God loves you and takes care of you.

— Psalm 91:11

31 Jesus Is with Me Morse Code

OBJECTIVE: To help children know the Lord is with them when they share the Gospel

Appropriate for ages 8 to 12

In some places missionaries use the Morse Code to send messages to one another. God has a special message for you to remember when you tell others about Jesus.

Use the code to read the message. Place the correct letter in the blank above each code. The solution is on page 64.

MORSE CODE

A	B	C	D	E	F	G	H	I	J	K	L
.-	-...	-.-.	-..	.	..-.	--.	....	..	.---	-.-	.-..

M	N	O	P	Q	R	S	T	U	V	W	Y
--	-.	---	.--.	--.-	.-.	...	-	..-	...-	.--	-.--

— Matthew 28:20

52 Ways to Teach Children to Share the Gospel   39

32   A Bag Full of Prayers

OBJECTIVE: A craft to encourage children to pray for missionaries

Appropriate for ages 6 to 12

Pray ye therefore the Lord of the harvest.
— Matthew 9:38

God's work is accomplished by prayer. Our missionaries need and depend on the prayers of God's people in order to spread the message of salvation. When you pray for missionaries you are choosing to serve the Lord.

What you need:
- crayons or felt pen
- scissors
- hole punch
- glue
- paper lunch-size sack, brown or blue
- 4 notebook paper reinforcements
- 14-inch piece of yarn

What to do:
1. Color the world map and the memory verse box from below and cut them out.
2. Center and paste the map on the paper sack.
3. Fold the top edge of the sack down about two inches to make a cuff.
4. Glue the memory verse on the cuff, above the world map.
5. Punch two holes, about three inches apart, through the cuff, on the back side of the bag.
6. Stick a notebook paper reinforcement on each side of each hole in the cuff.
7. Thread a piece of yarn through the holes and tie it to make a hanger.
8. Hang the bag in a place where you will see it often.

9. Collect missionary prayer requests from church bulletins, magazines, and letters from missionaries. Also, you may want to include prayer requests from your pastor, evangelist, your Sunday school teacher, and friends who are trying to be a witness for Christ.

10. Develop a habit of praying for missionaries all over the world. Choose a different prayer request from your bag each day.

Pray ye therefore the Lord of the harvest.
— Matthew 9:38

33   The Prayer Line

Appropriate for ages 8 to 12

God's work is done by prayer. We are dependent upon God's help to share the Gospel. The Prayer Line is always open. You never get a busy signal, and the conversation can be private. God wants you to talk with Him each day.

Read Jeremiah 33:3. Then, close your Bible and see if you can complete the message below. The number tells you which button on the phone contains the letter that belongs in each blank. The solution is on page 64.

Prayer Time:
Say a prayer to God right now and ask Him for His help for your needs. Then ask Him to help you share the Gospel with people you know who do not know Jesus.

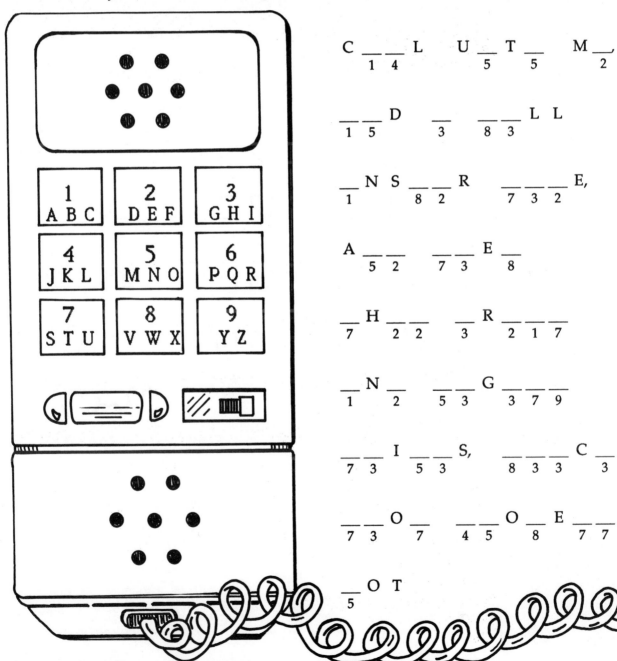

C __ __ L   U __ T __   M __,
  1 4   5   5   2

__ __ D   __   __ __ L L
1 5   3   8 3

__ N S __ __ R   __ __ __ E,
1   8 2   7 3 2

A __ __   __ __ E __
  5 2   7 3 8

__ H __ __   __ R __ __ __
7 2 2   3 2 1 7

__ N __   __ __ G __ __ __
1 2   5 3 3 7 9

__ __ I __ __ S,   __ __ __ C __
7 3 5 3   8 3 3 3

__ __ O __   __ __ O __ E __ __
7 3 7   4 5 8 7 7

__ O T
5

34 Encouraging Words

Appropriate for ages 8 to 12

OBJECTIVE: To teach children Scripture by which they can be encouraged in their service for the Lord, and share that Scripture with others

People who share the Gospel need lots of encouragement. It is not always easy to tell others about Jesus.

A good verse to share with others is I Thessalonians 5:24. Also, it is a good verse for you to remember as you serve the Lord where you are.

Break the code to discover what the verse says. Double-check the answer by looking it up in your Bible. The answer is on page 64.

F	A	O
S	E	T
H	I	W

—I Thessalonians 5:24

35

A Letter of Encouragement

OBJECTIVE: To help children write an encouraging letter to people having hard times

Appropriate for ages 8 to 12

Be strong and of a good courage; be not afraid, neither be thou dismayed: for the Lord thy God is with thee whithersoever thou goest.
— Joshua 1:9

Write a letter to encourage a friend or relative who is going through a hard time or a missionary in another country.

Describe some of your activities, what's happening in your family, and events at your church. Share Joshua 1:9. Remind your friend not to be afraid and let him know that the Lord is with him.

— — — — — — — — — — — — — **Cut Here** — — — — — — — — — — — — —

Dear _____,

_____

_____

_____

_____

_____

_____

_____

_____

_____

_____

_____

_____

Your friend,

_____

36 An Airmail Maze

OBJECTIVE: To remind children to write encouraging letters to others

Appropriate for ages 7 to 12

Friends and relatives going through hard times and missionaries struggling with difficulties need encouragement from praying friends. Find Joshua 1:9 in your Bible, and read it aloud. This is a good verse to share with a person experiencing difficulty. You may want to include this verse when you write to them.

Write the name of a friend, relative, or a missionary on the envelope. Then, write the name of the country or city where he lives on the picture of the world. Begin at the envelope and trace a path to the country or city of the person to whom you will be writing.

The solution is on page 64.

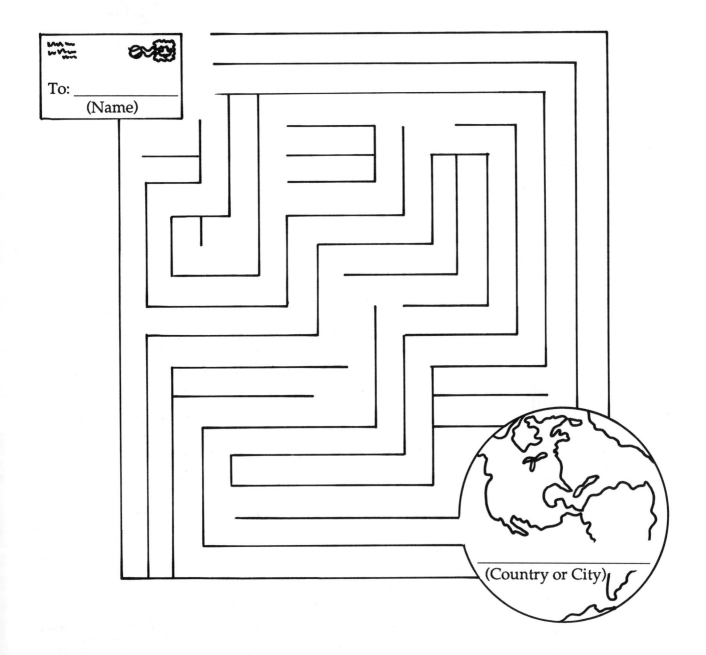

To: _____
(Name)

(Country or City)

37 Chosen Crossword

OBJECTIVE: To learn what God's Word says about being chosen to serve Him

Appropriate for ages 8 to 12

Everyone likes to be chosen. Missionaries choose to serve God and are chosen by Him.

You can choose to serve God, too. Read Joshua 24:15 (King James Version). Not only do you choose to serve Him, but you are chosen by the Lord. Read Jesus' Words in John 15:16.

Use these two Bible verses as clues to solve the crossword puzzle. The answers are on page 64.

ACROSS

1. The Lord tells us that He chooses us in the book of _____.
3. Who said, "I have chosen you?"
6. Not only are we to bear fruit, but that fruit should _____.
8. When you pray in Jesus' name, God will _____ you whatever you ask.
9. Choose you this day whom you will _____.

DOWN

1. What book of the Bible says that we have to choose whom we will serve?
2. You are chosen and ordained that you should _____.
4. _____ you this day whom you will serve.
5. The Lord chooses us so that we will bring forth _____.
7. We will ask the Father in Jesus' _____.

38 Needs of the Heart

OBJECTIVE: To have the children find and read Bible verses about heart-felt needs

Appropriate for ages 8 to 12

People everywhere have the same needs. They need to hear and know God's Word. They need to have opportunities to accept Jesus as their Savior. Each heart below represents a need. Look up each Bible reference and read the verse aloud. Match the correct Bible reference heart with the verse by drawing a red line or gluing a chenille wire to connect them. The answers are on page 64.

Fearful
Psalm 34:4

Jealous
Hebrews 13:5

Sinful
I John 1:9

1. If we confess our sins, He is faithful and just to forgive us our sins, and to cleanse us from all unrighteousness.

2. He healeth the broken in heart, and bindeth up their wounds.

3. Let not your heart be troubled: ye believe in God, believe also in Me.

4. I sought the Lord, and He heard me, and delivered me from all my fears.

5. Let your conversation be without covetousness; and be content with such things as ye have: for He hath said, "I will never leave thee, nor forsake thee."

6. And God shall wipe away all tears from their eyes; and there shall be no more death, neither sorrow, nor crying, neither shall there be any more pain: for the former things are passed away.

7. Be careful for nothing; but in every thing by prayer and supplication with thanksgiving let your requests be made known unto God. And the peace of God, which passeth all understanding, shall keep your hearts and minds through Christ Jesus.

Broken
Psalm 147:3

Worried
Philippians 4:6-7

Troubled
John 14:1

Sad
Revelation 21:4

Gospel Mobile

OBJECTIVE: To show children what they can do to spread the Gospel

Appropriate for ages 5 to 10

For we are labourers together with God.
— I Corinthians 3:9

Make a Gospel Mobile to remind you of three ways you can serve the Lord and spread the Gospel.

Try doing each of these things this week: share the Gospel with a friend, pray, and give your time or money to a project or missionary to help spread the Gospel.

What you need:
- scissors
- hole punch
- 4 yarn pieces cut into 12- and 14-inch lengths
- bright poster board
- glue

What to do:
1. Glue the patterns onto poster board.
2. Cut out the patterns.
3. Punch holes in the patterns as shown.
4. Attach a length of yarn to the top of the globe for a hanger.
5. Attach the other patterns to the bottom of the globe using various lengths of yarn.

GIVE
God loveth a cheerful giver.
— II Corinthians 9:7

PRAY
Pray ye therefore the Lord of the harvest, that He will send forth labourers into His harvest.
— Matthew 9:38

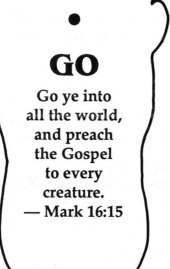

GO
Go ye into all the world, and preach the Gospel to every creature.
— Mark 16:15

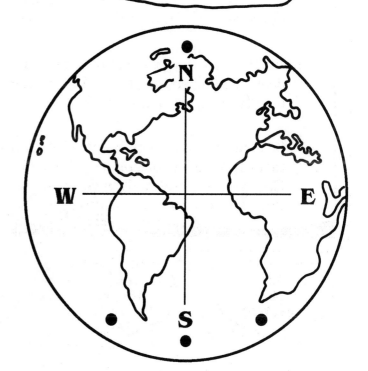

W E
N
S

40 Hut Bank

OBJECTIVE: To encourage children to give money to support missions projects

Appropriate for ages 6 to 12

For God loves a cheerful giver.
— II Corinthians 9:7 (NIV)

One way you can help spread the Gospel into all the world is to give of your money to help support missions projects.

The Hut Bank will remind you to save money for these special projects.

What you need:

- 1 16-oz empty cake frosting container without the lid, cleaned and dried
- half a letter-size manila file folder
- a 12 x 3 ½-inch sheet of brown construction paper
- stapler
- scissors
- glue
- pencil
- brown or black crayon
- straw, Spanish moss, or wood shavings

What to do:

1. Glue the brown construction paper around the frosting container and let it dry.

2. With a pencil, draw a doorway on the brown paper. Color the doorway.

3. Cut out the roof pattern.

4. Trace the roof pattern onto the manila folder.

5. Overlap the roof pattern to make a point at the top. Staple.

6. Glue straw, Spanish moss, or wood shavings on the roof.

7. Place the roof on top of the frosting container.

8. Remove and replace the roof each time you put money in the bank.

9. Give your offering CHEERFULLY!

Completed Bank

Fishing for Men

OBJECTIVE: To learn Scriptures encouraging obedience to God's Word and being a witness

Appropriate for ages 6 to 10

Ye shall be witnesses unto me.
— Acts 1:8

Christians in the Early Church met secretly and used the sign of the fish to let others know they belonged to Jesus. You can let others know you are a Christian. One way of showing that you love Jesus is by being obedient to His Word.

What you need:
- scissors
- glue
- crayons

What to do:
1. Color and cut out each fish in the water. (Do not cut out the "glue here" fish.)
2. Look up the Bible references on each fish.
3. Glue the fish with the correct reference beside the verse.
4. On the lines below each verse write a way you can show you are a Christian. The answers are on page 64.

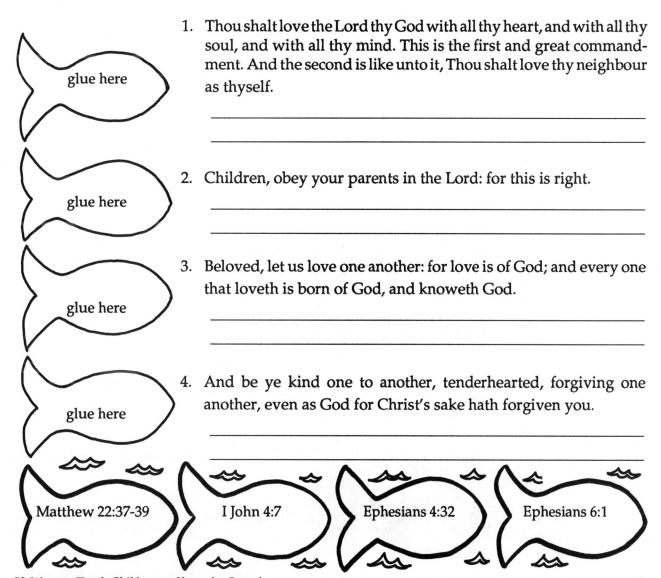

1. Thou shalt love the Lord thy God with all thy heart, and with all thy soul, and with all thy mind. This is the first and great commandment. And the second is like unto it, Thou shalt love thy neighbour as thyself.

_____

_____

2. Children, obey your parents in the Lord: for this is right.

_____

_____

3. Beloved, let us love one another: for love is of God; and every one that loveth is born of God, and knoweth God.

_____

_____

4. And be ye kind one to another, tenderhearted, forgiving one another, even as God for Christ's sake hath forgiven you.

_____

_____

Matthew 22:37-39   I John 4:7   Ephesians 4:32   Ephesians 6:1

42 Letter to a Friend

OBJECTIVE: To give children a practical way to share the Lord with a friend

Appropriate for ages 7 to 12

Declare . . . His wonders among all people.
— Psalm 96:3

People who go to other countries are not the only ones who are to tell others about Jesus. All believers are to be witnesses where they live. You can tell others about the Lord.

Write a letter to a friend telling something good the Lord has done for you.

- - - - - - - - - - - - - - - - Cut Here - - - - - - - - - - - - - - - -

Dear _____,

_____

_____

_____

_____

_____

_____

_____

_____

_____

_____

_____

_____

Your friend,

_____

43 Fish Stationery

OBJECTIVE: To help children share with others that they belong to Jesus.

Appropriate for ages 8 to 12

Ye shall be witnesses unto me.
— Acts 1:8

You can be a missionary and witness for Christ today. Writing letters is one way of sharing God's love with others.

Follow the instructions below and make your own fish-symbol stationary. Then, write a letter telling others that you belong to the Lord.

What you need:
- half a potato
- paring or carving knife
- sheets of white paper
- tempera paint
- letter-size envelopes

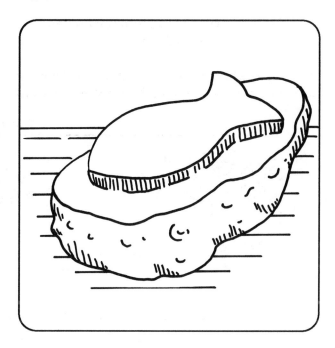

What to do:
1. Carve a fish outline in one half of the potato. Cut away the potato around the outside of the fish so that the fish symbol stands out
2. Dip the carved symbol in tempera paint and stamp it on the paper.
3. Follow the same procedure to stamp the envelopes.

More fun things to do:
1. Carve other Christian symbols like a cross or dove on the potato.
2. Make your own wrapping paper by stamping the symbols on tissue paper.

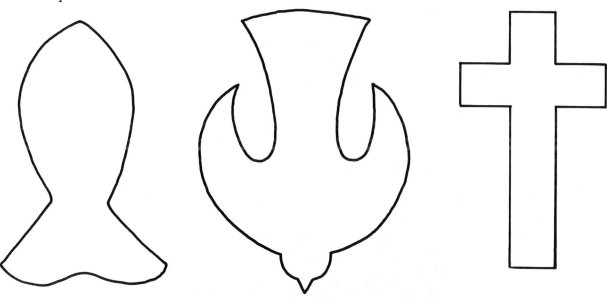

Being a Witness

OBJECTIVE: To teach children a Bible verse encouraging them to be witnesses for Christ

Appropriate for ages 8 to teens

Jesus told His disciples that they would be witnesses unto Him. Use the code to see what the verse says. Doublecheck your answer by looking it up in the Bible (New International Version). The answer is on page 64. This promise is still true today. We can be witnesses for Jesus right now where we live, and maybe someday in other parts of the world.

A	B	C	D	E	F	G	H	I	J	K	L	M	N	O	P	Q
1	2	3	4	5	6	7	8	9	10	11	12	13	14	15	16	17

R	S	T	U	V	W	X	Y	Z
18	19	20	21	22	23	24	25	26

```
 2  21  20      25  15  21      24   9  12  12      18   5   3   5   9  22   5

16  15  23   5  18      23   8   5  14      20   8   5      8  15  12  25

19  16   9  18   9  20       3  15  13   5  19      15  14      25  15  21 ;

 1  14   4      25  15  21      24   9  12  12       2   5      13  25

23   9  20  14   5  19  19   5  19       9  14

10   5  18  21  19   1  12   5  13 ,    1  14   4       9  14       1  12  12

10  21   4   5   1       1  14   4      19   1  13   1  18   9   1       1  14   4

20  15      20   8   5       5  14   4  19      15   6      20   8   5

 5   1  18  20   8 .
```

— Acts 1:8 (NIV)

45 Reflecting His Light

OBJECTIVE: To teach children what God's Word says about letting their lights shine for Him

Appropriate for ages 7 to 12

Being a witness for Christ is a continuous task. Where we go, what we do, and what we say tell others that we love and serve Him.

Jesus gave us a special message in Matthew 5:16 about letting our lights shine for Him.

Hold the candle up to a mirror. Read the message as it is being reflected in the mirror.

Other people will see what Jesus is like by what they see in your actions and by the words they hear you say.

You Are the Light

OBJECTIVE: To reinforce the importance of sharing the Gospel outside the church

Appropriate for ages 8 to 12

You are the light of the world.
— Matthew 5:14 (NIV)

When we go to church we go to worship God. We learn God's Word and how to share it with others. In Matthew 5:14 Jesus calls His disciples the "light of the world." Help the boy let his light shine in his world.

Solve the math problem in the church. The answer will tell you which numbered area to go to next.

Draw a line from the church to that area. Continue until the boy reaches his friends. The answer to the math problem in the final candle will be the number of disciples Jesus had. The answers are on page 64.

3. Visiting a Sick Person

9. At the Park

5. With Friends

1. Church

16. At School

2. At the Mall

15. At the Store

8. At Home

52 Ways to Teach Children to Share the Gospel

 **Go & Be a Witness**

OBJECTIVE: To help children relate and apply scriptural principles to life situations

Appropriate for ages 8 to 12
2 to 6 players

Cut apart the rectangles below and glue each one onto a 3 x 5-inch card. Divide into teams of two to six players. Give each team a set of cards. Scramble the cards and have each player pick one.

Have each player read the card and describe how he can be a witness for Christ to the people in the situation he has just read about. Then, have the player read the Bible references aloud. Continue until each player has had a turn.

Be a Witness and Go

to a boy or girl who has just moved into your neighborhood.

What Can You Do or Say?

God's Word says:
   Luke 14:23
   Mark 12:31

Be a Witness and Go

to a family in your community whose house burned down.

What Can You Do or Say?

God's Word says:
   Philippians 4:13, 19
   Philippians 4:6-7

Be a Witness and Go

to a classmate that no one likes.

What Can You Do or Say?

God's Word says:
   I John 4:7
   I John 4:11-12

Be a Witness and Go

to a Christian friend who doesn't take the time to read his Bible.

What Can You Do or Say?

God's Word says:
   Psalm 119:9, 11
   Colossians 3:16

Be a Witness and Go

to a lonely, old woman who lives on your street.

What Can You Do or Say?

God's Word says:
   Hebrews 13:5-6
   Psalm 68:6

Be a Witness and Go

to a friend at school who said you cheated on the last math test, even though you didn't.

What Can You Do or Say?

God's Word says:
   Ephesians 4:32; Matthew 6:14, 15
   Matthew 5:44

---

48 Go into Your World

OBJECTIVE: To help children learn and apply Matthew 28:19-20

Appropriate for ages 8 to 12
2 to 6 players

Make a game board by duplicating pages 57 and 58. Glue the pages onto the inside of a manila file folder. Cover the game with adhesive-backed plastic for added durability.

Duplicate the cards below six times for each game set. Shuffle the cards and place them face down in the center of the game board. Use assorted buttons for markers.

52 Ways to Teach Children to Share the Gospel

"GO into all the world." Take an additional turn.	Sing "Jesus Loves Me" in Spanish: Si Cristo me ama (3X) La Biblia dice asi.		Say your favorite Bible verse out loud.

Love thy neighbor.

Have you asked Jesus into your ♡? **If your answer is *yes*, tell us when.**

Playing Instructions

Each player places a button on START. The first player draws one card and moves his button the number of squares shown. If he lands on a picture square he is to tell something he can do in that situation that shows he is a witness for Jesus.

If he lands on a word square, he must follow the instructions before his next turn. The first player to reach the FINISH square wins. The FINISH square must be reached by an exact count.

Glue Page 58 Here

GO Into Your

Read I John 5:11-12 aloud from your Bible.		Say John 3:16 from memory (if you can't, choose someone in your class to say it).	

Share something good the Lord has done for you.

FINISH
Clap your hands 3 times, then say, *Amen!*

START
Go Ye
Read
Matthew 28:19-20

Place **CARDS** here

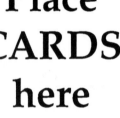

Say to the person on your left, "Jesus loves you."

World

Sing a song about Jesus.

Pretend you are playing a trombone.

Tell the person on your right, "Jesus is the Way, the Truth, and the Life."

Cut Here

49 Sing unto the Lord

OBJECTIVE: To teach children the meaning of Psalm 96:2 and help them apply it to their lives

Appropriate for ages 6 to 12

Read Psalm 96. This Psalm is an invitation for the whole earth to sing unto the Lord. This can only happen if people spread the Gospel to other children, nations, tribes, and races.

Close your Bible. To complete the verse, write the name of each note in the blanks below. Open your Bible to check the completed verse. The solution is on page 64.

Talk about it:

Share one good thing the Lord has done for you. This is one way of following Psalm 96:2.

CODE KEY

E G B D F   F A C E

Sin__ unto th__ Lord, __l__ss

His n_m__; show __orth His

s__lv__tion __rom d__y to __ay.

— Ps__lm 96:2

50 Psalm 96 Choral Reading

OBJECTIVE: To teach children a Scripture passage with an emphasis on witnessing

Appropriate for ages 6 to 12

Duplicate this page for each child. Divide the children into a boys section and a girls section. Select four persons for the solo parts, and read Psalm 96 as a speech choir.

Psalm 96 is a call to worship for all nations. As the Gospel is spread into all the earth, many nationalities have come to know the Lord.

You can be a part in spreading the Gospel by praying, giving money to support missionaries, and by telling your friends about Jesus.

ALL: O sing unto the Lord a new song: sing unto the Lord, all the earth. Sing unto the Lord, bless His name; show forth His salvation from day to day.

BOYS: Declare His glory among the heathen, His wonders among all people.

SOLO 1: For the Lord is great, and greatly to be praised: He is to be feared above all gods.

SOLO 2: For all the gods of the nations are idols: but the Lord made the heavens.

GIRLS: Honour and majesty are before Him: strength and beauty are in His sanctuary.

BOYS: Give unto the Lord, O ye kindreds of the people, give unto the Lord glory and strength. Give unto the Lord the glory due unto His name: bring an offering, and come into His courts.

GIRLS: O worship the Lord in the beauty of holiness: fear before him, all the earth.

SOLO 3: Say among the heathen that the Lord reigneth: the world also shall be established that it shall not be moved: He shall judge the people righteously.

SOLO 4: Let the heavens rejoice, and let the earth be glad; let the sea roar, and the fulness thereof.

BOYS: Let the field be joyful, and all that is therein: then shall all the trees of the wood rejoice before the Lord:

ALL: For He cometh, for He cometh to judge the earth: He shall judge the world with righteousness, and the people with His Truth.

Another Fun Thing to Do:
- After the choral reading, divide into small groups and act out one way you can share the Gospel. Talk about each group's skit. Would this be a way of sharing the Gospel at school, at church, or at home? Has anyone in your goup ever tried it? Think of other things you could do to share the Gospel with someone.

Hidden Salvation Messages

OBJECTIVE: To review and learn Scripture passages about salvation

Appropriate for ages 7 to 12

Missionaries go and tell the message of salvation so others will believe and come to know Jesus as Savior. There is a message in the puzzle below that tells us how we can be saved and have eternal life. It is a message for you, and it is a message for you to tell someone else.

Have you memorized John 3:16? It is hidden in the puzzle. It reads from left to right, row by row, but there are other words included. Underline the words of John 3:16. You may use your Bible (New International Version) if you're not sure of the exact words. When you finish, the words that do not belong in John 3:16 make up another verse about salvation found in Acts 16:31. The verses appear on page 64.

FOR GOD BELIEVE IN SO
LOVED THE THE LORD
WORLD THAT HE GAVE
JESUS HIS ONE AND ONLY
AND SON YOU THAT WILL
WHOEVER BELIEVES BE IN
HIM SAVED SHALL NOT
PERISH YOU AND BUT
HAVE YOUR ETERNAL
HOUSEHOLD LIFE

52 John 3:16 Garland

OBJECTIVE: A craft to remind children of God's love for all the people of the world

Appropriate for ages 8 to 12

For God so loved the world that He gave His one and only Son, that whoever believes in Him shall not perish but have eternal life.
— John 3:16 (NIV)

Because God loves all the people of the world, we need to let everyone hear the Good News of salvation. As you see your finished garland, it will be a reminder to you to pray for your friends who need to hear the Gospel.

What you need:
- construction paper or poster board, red, brown, yellow, black, white, & pink
- scissors
- pen or marker
- white craft glue
- 1 yard of ½-inch wide grosgrain ribbon

What to do:
1. Cut out the heart pattern, and trace around it on pink (or red) construction paper. Make six hearts.
2. On each heart write one word of the first six words of John 3:16.
3. Cut out the child pattern, and trace around it on each of the other colors of construction paper: red (or pink), brown, yellow, black, and white. Cut them out.
4. Alternate placing the hearts and children on the ribbon. Try to leave quite a bit of empty ribbon at each end.
5. Glue the hearts and children on the ribbon.

6. Tie a knot or a bow on each end of the remaining ribbon.
7. Hang the garland in a place where you will enjoy it. It will remind you to pray for your friends and to tell them of God's great love for all people.

More fun things to do:
- Make several of these garlands to hang on your Christmas tree.
- Write the name of a missionary and his or her country on each child pattern. Pray for a different missionary each week.
- Make several missionary garlands and give them as gifts, so others will be reminded to pray for missionaries too.

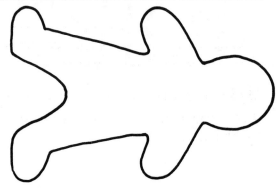

Answer Page

1 Alphabet Code Fun, Page 7

For God so loved the world that He gave His one and only Son, that whoever believes in Him shall not perish but have eternal life. — John 3:16 (NIV)

3 His Last Command, Page 9

Therefore go and make disciples of all nations, baptizing them in the name of the Father and of the Son and of the Holy Spirit, and teaching them to obey everything I have commanded you. And surely I am with you always, to the very end of the age. — Matthew 28:19-20 (NIV)

6 Manger Message, Page 12

He Himself bore our sins in His body on the tree, so that we might die to sins and live for righteousness; by His wounds you have been healed. — I Peter 2:24 (NIV)

7 Christmas Tree Poem, Page 13

tree, Jesus, me, voice, sing, Son, King

8 Go with the Gospel, Page 14

Go ye into all the world, and preach the Gospel to every creature. — Mark 16:15

11 Fruit of the Spirit, Page 17

1. love   2. joy   3. peace
4. longsuffering   5. gentleness   6. goodness
7. faith   8. meekness   9. temperance

12 Jesus Is the Way, Page 18

Jesus saith unto him, "I am the Way, the Truth, and the Life: no man cometh unto the Father, but by Me." — John 14:6

15 The Good News-Paper, Page 22

God, loved, world, Son, believeth, everlasting, life — John 3:16
all, sinned, God — Romans 3:23

---

sin, death — Romans 6:23
salvation, none, men, saved — Acts 4:12
Way, Truth, Life, Me — John 14:6
received, sons, believe — John 1:12
eternal, life, Son, life, Son — I John 5:11-12

17 Psalm of Gladness, Page 24

Make a joyful noise unto the Lord, all ye lands. Serve the Lord with gladness. — Psalm 100:1-2

19 Before I Come Back Skit, Page 26

1. clean   5. pleased or happy
2. Mother   6. Bible
3. helped   7. obey
4. obeyed   8. Gospel

20 Jesus' Last Command, Page 27

1. And He said unto them, "Go ye into all the world, and preach the Gospel to every creature."
2. into all the world
   preach the Gospel to everyone

23 World-Wide Word Search, Page 30

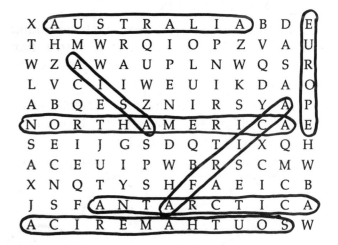

26 Sent by Jesus Braille Code, Page 34

As My Father hath sent Me, even so send I you. — John 20:21

28 Pray with Understanding, Page 36

1. Bible reading & prayer
2. climate
3. culture
4. health
5. language
6. loneliness
7. relationships with others
8. safety in danger
9. travel

31 Jesus Is with Me Morse Code, Page 39

And, lo, I am with you always, even unto the end of the world. — Matthew 28:20

33 The Prayer Line, Page 41

Call unto me, and I will answer thee, and show thee great and mighty things, which thou knowest not. — Jeremiah 33:3

34 An Encouraging Word, Page 42

Faithful is He that calleth you, who also will do it. — I Thessalonians 5:24

36 A Maze of Encouragement, Page 44

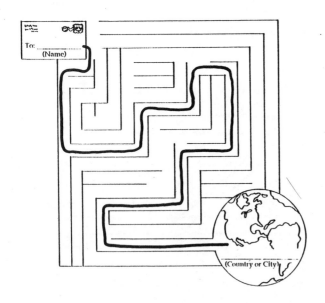

37 Choosing and Being Chosen, Page 45

Across
1. John
3. Jesus
6. remain
8. give
9. serve

Down
1. Joshua
2. go
4. choose
5. fruit
7. name

38 Needs of the Heart, Page 46

1. I John 1:9
2. Psalm 147:3
3. John 14:1
4. Psalm 34:4
5. Hebrews 13:5
6. Revelation 21:4
7. Philippians 4:6-7

41 Fishing for Men, Page 49

1. Matthew 22:37-39
2. Ephesians 6:1
3. I John 4:7
4. Ephesians 4:32

44 Being a Witness, Page 52

But you will receive power when the Holy Spirit comes on you; and you will be My witnesses in Jerusalem, and in all Judea and Samaria, and to the ends of the earth. — Acts 1:8 (NIV)

46 You Are the Light, Page 54

8, 9, 16, 2, 3, 15, 5, 12

49 Sing unto the Lord, Page 59

Sing unto the Lord, bless His name; show forth His salvation from day to day. — Psalm 96:2

51 Hidden Salvation Verses, Page 61

For God so loved the world that He gave His one and only Son that whoever believes in Him shall not perish but have eternal life. — John 3:16 (NIV)

Believe in the Lord Jesus, and you will be saved — you and your household. — Acts 16:31 (NIV)